Dark, Light and

Powerful Poetry

From the Heart of a Fallen Angel

By

Timothy J Chisholm

Dear Joe

Here's to Living Life
Be it Dark, Light or Twilight

Timothy J

Dedicated to my beautiful partner Barham, and to my wonderful children, Cameron & Zahra.

With love to my brother Andrew, and to my sister Caroline.

With special thanks to Wilf Hashimi and to Hilary Porter BA (Hons), First Class.

Foreword

Firstly, may I wish you a very warm welcome and thank you for purchasing my poetry.

The following pages contain all of my finished work: from 2004 – 2017 inclusive. I have always had a leaning towards direct, raw and emotional poetry. Direct from the heart, through the pen, onto the page.

I like to read a poem in the morning, get the initial emotion from it, and then let it sink in. Over the course of the day, I will revisit it. Reading all or part of it again, allowing my understanding of the piece to grow. Its full meaning, to me, will be revealed over time.

I would liken reading poetry, to savouring a fine wine. I would never rush it. For me, a good poem, deserves a day of my life. A good bottle of wine deserves a few hours.

You will be pleased to know that you can interact with me via my Facebook page: **Tim Chisholm – Poet and Author.**

I paint the pictures of my mind,

With carefully chosen phrases,

Using the brush strokes of my pen,

To draw a heartbeat,

From these lifeless pages.

This is artistry of the mind,

It's what you see, and no-one else,

Take from it, all that you desire,

Then place it back,

Gently,

Upon the shelf.

Bookmark Your Favourite Poems Below

(Create your own personal index)

Poem	Page	Notes

Bookmark Your Favourite Poems Below

(Create your own personal index)

Poem   **Page**   **Notes**

The Call of the Oystercatcher

(Port Bannatyne)

The call of the oystercatcher and nothing more,

As I sit in silence on Port Bannatyne shore,

The sea rests with me, shimmering and calm,

Soothing furrowed brow, with mesmeric charm.

The scent of the seaweed, pleases the air,

As I breathe deeply - in with relief and out with despair,

The gentleness of the breeze, upon my weary cheek,

Soft as the mother's touch, that I still seek.

The soul, bathed in beauty, immersion complete,

As I savour the last moments and linger, before I retreat,

The restoration of peace, acknowledged and greatly received,

Serenity, returned to its rightful owner, no longer bereaved.

Unique

We may travel the same path,

We may walk side by side, for some of the journey,

We may even have the same final destination,

But.....

We will each leave our own footprints.

Silent Echo

Eventually, we are all lost, to time,

Eventually, we all become, mere memories,

Eventually, anything we did, becomes the forgotten ripple,

Of a solitary stone, thrown into the vast ocean, of all our yesterdays,

Everything we once thought, has evaporated,

Like the early morning dew, touched by sunlight,

And we are returned to cosmic dust, once again.

Occasionally, we are remembered,

Occasionally, a random reincarnation, draws a smile or a tear,

Occasionally, something we did, resurrects, resurfaces,

A thought we had, a phrase we uttered, revisited by those held dear,

A tear, distilled over time, by the cooling of warm thoughts for a loved one,

Drops into the salt water ocean, made from the tears, of all our tomorrows,

And a faint ripple forms: a silent echo, of a solitary, timeless, stone.

Live to Fear Another Day

Have you ever thought you're different?

But don't know why,

Have you ever thought whose life is this?

And begun to cry,

Have you ever tried listening to yourself?

And been unable to hear,

Have you ever felt you're losing your mind?

As you wiped away that tear.

Have you ever touched the gates of Hell?

But never wandered in,

Have you ever thought that you are evil?

And remembered every sin,

Have you ever become chained to your past?

And been unable to find the key,

Have you ever felt the birds don't sing?

And the sun doesn't shine on me.

Have you ever craved love so much?

But found so little shown,

Have you ever felt you're still a child?

But know that you have grown,

Have you ever been hurt, by those you love?

Yet thought, you must be bad,

Have you always suffered in silence?

To spare others from seeing you sad.

Have you ever heard the sound of anger?

And recognised that voice,

Have you ever wished that you could leave?

But found you had no choice,

Have you ever been so frightened?

And unable to get away,

Have you ever had to hide yourself?

To live, to fear another day.

Dark and Light

Darkness falls across my face,

In this cold and empty place,

In death's waiting room,

I stand alone.

In this cold and empty place,

I feel no favour or disgrace,

And have no urge,

To wander home.

In death's waiting room I stand,

No one here to hold my hand,

I pass through darkness,

Until light.

I emerge, new flesh and bone,

Distant memories have all gone,

Once again, I am,

Devoid of plight.

Darkness falls across my face,

Wrapped in sheets as fine as lace,

Once again, I cry,

To fill my lungs.

Into The Dark

Darkened by the loss of life,
Darkened by the fall of night,
Darkened by the hand of death,
Drawing darker with his last breath.

Darker by the angel's side,
Darker thoughts within his mind,
Darker nightmares full of fear,
Drawing darkness ever near.

Darkness falls across his form,
Darkness deep and so forlorn,
Darkness steals from him today,
Drawing his darkened soul away.

Journey

We are tourists of the present,

Led by ghosts of our past,

Towards a future of uncertainty,

On a journey that doesn't last.

Make the Dawn

Into the darkest hour,

Where demons fear to tread,

Into the darkest hour,

Since you were born.

Into the darkest hour,

Where your mind is fed,

On raw emotion, fear and scorn.

Into the darkest hour,
Where no words can be said,
Into the darkest hour,
Lost, alone and forlorn.

Into the darkest hour,
Where you will meet your death,
Unless you make the dawn.

Know

Talk of good times,

And not sorrow,

But know that sorrow exists,

Think of memories,

That you do not borrow,

But know what you will miss.

Corrupted by Twilight

The day and the night,

Separate and yet,

Both shadow and light,

When you enter dusk or dawn

A mind full of sight,

Intelligent and yet,

Confused wrong and right,

When you enter dusk or dawn

A sky blue and bright,

Clear and yet,

Clouded by your plight,

When you enter dusk or dawn

A man full of might,

Strong and yet,

Weakened by the fight,

When you enter dusk or dawn

A life pure and white,

Innocent and yet,

Corrupted by twilight,

When you enter dusk or dawn

Stripped

A man stripped of all his possessions,

Is left but one thing,

His Dignity,

Until his own death

A man stripped of all his clothes,

Is left but one thing,

His Innocence,

Until his last breath

A man stripped of all his flesh,

Is left but one thing,

His Soul,

Even after he dies

But….

A man stripped of all his emotions,

Is left but nothing,

He is lost,

Until he cries.

My Prayer

Give me the courage to endure

Everything that I must,

Give me the wisdom to secure

A life that is true and just

Give me the tolerance to hear

What others have to say,

Give me the drive to clear

My path along the way

Give me the heart to embrace

All that I have to do,

Give me the character to face

A future chosen by few

Give me the compassion to care

For those who need to heal,

Give me the humility to share

My wealth, my home, my meal

Give me the honesty to say

When I am not right,

Give me the strength to walk away

When others seek to fight

Give me the will to succeed

In helping others see the sun,

Give me the decency to need

Nothing for all I have done

Give me the confidence to leave

My tears for all to see,

Give me the reason to believe

I have the right to be

Give me the power to see

Not just the gift of sight,

Give me the honour to be

Trusted to do what is right.

Close Your Eyes

Close your eyes, for you are weary,

Close your eyes and think of me,

Close your eyes, drift peacefully,

Close your eyes.

Close your eyes, you need your rest,

Close your eyes, with your heart caressed,

Close your eyes, hope for the best,

Close your eyes.

Close your eyes, when you're overcome,

Close your eyes, no harm will come,

Close your eyes, my precious one,

Close your eyes.

Close your eyes, to see the view,

Close your eyes, your dreams come true,

Close your eyes, I'm there with you,

Close your eyes.

15th December

Taken on a winter's eve,

Stolen under moonlit sky,

Taken from those you loved,

With no chance to say goodbye.

I am the thief who stole so much,

I am the thief who took your life,

I am the thief who will never forget,

That I stole a friend, a mother and a wife.

I am so very sorry.

Modern Masters

See the many faces, of hypocrisy,

See the modern masters and their slaves,

See them looking down, on you and me,

Silencing the many, by killing the brave.

Hear the twisted rhetoric of those born free,

Hear them espouse, what's best for us all,

Hear them blaming foreigners, you and me,

Treasuring their advance, with the pleasure of our fall.

Speak about your freedom and your liberty,

Speak about your honour and your pride,

Speak about your love of true honesty,

But know, unless you live them, you have already died.

Feel the heavy burden of your work and loan,

Feel the yolk tighten round muted throat,

Feel the need to nurture the seeds you have sown,

Or chain the next generation to the oars of this iniquitous boat.

Smell the rotting stench of the capitalist,

Smell the greed and envy that he exudes,

Smell the foulest creatures that we enlist,

To keep the poor in their place and the starving from their food.

Taste what is real and find your voice,

Taste your own medicine, that should be free,

Taste the bitter truth and use freedom of choice,

To break the wretched curse of this greed driven insanity.

Revolution
(Our Evolution. "R-evolution")

What if I should choose,

To play no part,

In this outdated game,

This ignoble charade?

What if I should move,

To depart,

From this life of blame,

And expose this facade?

What if I should remove,

The joker's hearts,

From this deck of shame,

And play, one final card?

That I should reprove,

These upstarts,

Using clubs and spades,

For the ultimate discard.

After I Have Passed

Should you have a choice,
Choose happiness,
After I have passed,
Life,
Is for the living,
Sadness,
Is but a mere shadow,
Cast,
By my fading light.

Should you have a choice,
Choose love,
After my celestial uplifting,
The heart,
Is for giving,
Sorrow,
Is but a lone cloud,
Drifting,
On a breeze of memories.

Angel

You are an Angel,

Come to earth,

To show me love,

You are divine inspiration,

From heaven above.

Awaken

Lie back in the sun or shade,

Lie back and relax all day,

Lie back with no cares,

Lie back and rest,

Lie back.

Sit up and watch the world go by,

Sit up and hear the planet cry,

Sit up and look around,

Sit up and feel,

Sit up.

Stand up for what you know to be right,

Stand up and be prepared to fight,

Stand up for your beliefs,

Stand up for good,

Stand up.

Tip-toe with respect around the dreams of others,

Paddle with love through the tears of your brothers,

March with hope towards peace,

Stride on with open heart,

Release.

All That is Real

Why wish for more?

When all that is real,

Is the here and now,

And no one can steal,

This moment from you.

Why grieve the past?

When all that is real,

Is the here and now,

And no-one can heal,

This torment but you.

Do not be distracted,

By longing for more,

Because all that is real,

Lay at your front door,

And no-one can steal,

This moment from you.

Do not re-enact it,

By grieving the past,

Because all that is real,

Was never made to last,

And no-one can heal,

This torment but you.

Magazines & Clock

Anxiously waiting,

Chewing fingers to the quick,

Nervously lamenting,

The wounds he could not lick.

Reluctantly accepting,

That his mind, is not his own,

Patiently sitting by himself,

Wishing that he was all alone.

Be Happy

Be happy that we met,

Be happy that we are still together,

Be happy that we have no regrets,

And that our love is pure, forever.

Be happy that we have endured bad times,

Be happy that together we are stronger,

Be happy that the mountains we have climbed,

Have made our love last ever longer.

Be happy that we have nothing to fear,

Be happy that together we have conquered all,

Be happy because I am always by your side,

And that I will never let you fall.

Autobiography

Why write a book so full of pain?

Why look back and try to explain?

Why sit over blank pages and stare?

Relive the hurt and remember despair?

Why must I show what it is to be me?

Because only then will I truly be free.

Black Pepper - Andrew

Black pepper on your starter young man?

The waiter holds the mill,

Yes, I love black pepper on everything,

So I surely will

Black pepper with your main course sir?

The waiter stands and waits,

Yes, yes, black pepper on everything,

Every single plate

Is everything fine my friend?

The waiter familiar and polite,

Yes, it's quite superb,

But….

More black pepper would be just right

Some port my good friend?

The waiter delivers the cheese,

Yes, 10 year old Otima,

And some black pepper please

Dessert wine my old friend?

The waiter brings strawberries for pud,

Yes, Brown's Orange Muscat,

And some black pepper would be good

The black pepper is near the end,

The mill breathes its last,

Like sand in an hourglass,

All his time had passed

At the service to remember,

In the "crem" upon the hill,

With all the mourners present,

A waiter with a pepper mill

Only nasty people he had met,

Were invited to his wake,

No family or friends welcome,

Was this a big mistake?

The old waiter greeted the guests,

Announcing the free feast,

If.....

You all use the pepper from this mill,

At the request of the deceased

The greedy people didn't care,

They ate and drank apace,

The emptied mill returned,

To its final resting place

Family and friends truly understood,

At the reading of his will,

His only wish….That at his wake,

He was in the pepper mill.

Be Yourself

Be good,

Be Happy,

Be strong,

Make a difference.

Clean the Slate

Does your mind pierce your heart,

With sharpened memories,

That you would rather forget?

Does your heart hold your tears to ransom,

Released only upon payment,

Of feeling sadness and regret?

Do your memories drag your past,

Oh so clearly,

Into today?

Do your tears clean the slate,

Of emotional debt,

That this life has made you pay?

Enough

Clouded mind so full of woe,

Leaves me unable to choose,

In which direction I should go,

While lethargy takes its dues.

Sitting behind the net curtain,

Staring in windowless confusion,

Everything seems far from certain,

But I come to the conclusion.....

I do not know what to do or say,

But that is enough,

Enough for today,

Enough.

Come Walk With Me

Nothing here is free?

Always a price to pay?

Come walk with me,

And open your eyes today.

The grass waving in the breeze,

So gentle and so calm,

Dappled shade from the trees,

Shadows dancing on your arm.

The sunset behind the hills,

The birds sing evensong,

All this with no bills,

Nature's music is never wrong.

The clouds gently waft,

Across light blue skies,

Water droplets from aloft,

Nature's price does not rise.

The fresh morning sky,

Air purified by trees,

The stars show on high,

And still there are no fees.

The planet is a gift,

To all of us it's free,

But only if you do not drift,

Past all there is to see.

Creation and Destruction

Who builds people up?

Who knocks them down?

Some have no cup,

Some wear a crown.

Should we all be the same?

Should we all survive?

Should some feel the shame,

For those no more alive?

Who has the power to decide?

Who goes on or is left behind,

Who pushes people off this ride?

Are they sick or are they blind?

Cupid – This Time

The first time you glance,

The first time you meet,

The first time you shake hands,

Just happy to greet.

The first time you hug,

The first time you part,

The second he leaves,

Tugs at your heart.

The second time you meet,

The first time you kiss,

The first time you think,

There could be more to this.

The third time you touch,

The first time you know,

Your heart beats so fast,

Your mind says go slow.

The fourth time for sure,

The first time feels right,

The first time you cherish,

Staying overnight.

The first Cupid's arrow,

Strikes your breast bone,

The second deep and true,

The last time you're alone.

Farewell and Not Goodbye

Oh little ones so small,

Why did God have to call,

All four of you away,

Before you saw one day.

Our love for you all,

Is no less or small,

I want you all to know,

That we all love you so.

Oh little ones so small,

Why did God have to call,

All four of you away,

Before we had a chance to play.

My four angels on high,

This is farewell and not goodbye,

At this time and in this place,

Daddy gives you a loving embrace.

Oh little ones so small,

Why did God have to call,

All four of you away,

Now is the time for me to say.....

Daddy Loves You All So Very Much.

See the love in Daddy's face,

As you rest in your final place,

I tuck you in and kiss you goodnight,

As God's hand turns out your light.

My Sweet Children

Now you are with your family,

No longer are you wandering,

Lost and alone,

Run and play my sweet children,

Run and play,

For you have all come home........

Today.

Days of Life

Days of loss,

Days of gain,

Days of happiness,

Days of pain.

Days of highs,

Days of lows,

Days of hiding,

Days of shows.

Days of laughs,

Days of tears,

Days of hopes,

Days of fears.

Days of giving,

Days of yearning,

Days of teaching,

Days of learning.

Days of loving,

Days of caring,

Days of living,

Days of sharing.

Days of feeling,

Days of knowing,

Days of seeing,

You are growing.

Death's Waiting Room

In death's waiting room,

Is where we all live..... and wait,

Some understand they are mortal,

Most are afforded little time,

To contemplate

Life leaves many distractions,

Manmade diversions in plentiful supply,

Making our lives, just too busy,

To genuinely remember,

Who was last to die.

Destiny

Who stole my life?

Who took it from me?

Who was the grim reaper?

Of my destiny.

A flash of light,

And I'm back at the scene,

Only I know,

What could have been.

Three precious lives,

Are what were lost,

Two died there,

But I carried the cost.

Distraction

Why must I suffer this endless self-inflicted torment?

Why continue to twist the knife until it is hell bent?

Should I indulge myself, With these awful thoughts?

Or forcefully distract my mind, From being so distraught?

Drawn to You

Oh beautiful woman,

Your smile so sweet,

Fills me with warmth,

Your face lights the sky,

Beauty beyond compare,

I am drawn to you,

With such force, I cannot resist,

Just to see you, fills me with joy,

To talk to you, I am in awe,

Never have I seen such beauty,

In my heart I know it cannot be,

I must go on alone,

Knowing I will never find another,

So perfect and pure,

Farewell.......

But you will not notice,

When I am gone,

For there is no room in your heart,

For me.

Dreams Without Reality

What are dreams without reality?

What is reality without dreams?

What if in this life,

Nothing is what it seems?

What are nights without a day?

What is day without night?

What if we cannot see,

Even with the gift of sight?

What are words without meaning?

What is meaning without words?

What if we cannot hear,

The singing of the birds?

What are thoughts without action?

What is action without thought?

What if we were free,

To live the life we sought?

What are feelings without emotion?

What is emotion without feeling?

What if we have no power,

To help our minds in healing?

What are teachers without a lesson?

What is a lesson without a teacher?

What if we can be holy,

Without the need of a preacher?

What are lovers without passion?

What is passion without love?

What if the fire,

Is lit from below and not above?

What are shadows without light?

What is light without shadow?

What if we need both,

For our feeble minds to grow?

What are dawns without a dusk?

What is dusk without dawn?

What if we must die,

So we can be reborn?

What are deaths without a life?

What is life without death?

What if we only understand,

After taking our last breath?

What are questions without an answer?

What is an answer without questions?

What can we forgive,

Everyone their transgressions?

What are wings without an angel?

What is an angel without wings?

What if you are a seraph,

From life eternal springs?

Dreams

Dream of days full of laughter,

Dream of happiness and love,

Dream of walking hand in hand,

Dream of nights full of passion,

Dream of sleeping in my arms,

Dream of waking next to me,

Dream of all these things,

And know......

That I share your dreams.

Driven

Driven by the dream of love,

Driven from the stars above,

Driven as the purest snow,

Driven until you let go.

Earth

Always giving what you need,

Look beyond the surface,

What do you see?

Everything is part of me.

England

Honoured Knights of this noble land,

Wearing true colours of red and white,

Stand firm for your sovereign England,

And show your courage to win the Fight.

First Date

Waiting at the station,

Alive with anticipation,

Lover, stranger or friend,

Who will fate dare to send?

First Meeting

Nothing lifts the heart like love,

The gentle caress of its power,

Strokes the mind with velvet glove,

A warm and sensual emotional shower.

Free Yourself

Who was it who said,

Death where is thy sting?

For those left behind,

It is in everything.

There is only so much grief,

One poor soul can bear,

Love maybe all around,

But death is everywhere.

The greatness of the loss,

Absolute and utter despair,

Abandoned for the rest of time,

With you no longer there.

My loving Mum and Dad,

You meant so much to me,

Both torn from my heart,

As I stood by helplessly.

I must free myself from torment,

Or dig an early grave,

Learn to cherish my own life,

For it's the only one, I can save.

Freedom

Freedom to choose, whatever you wish,

Freedom of thought,

Freedom to say no to anyone,

Is learned but never taught.

Freedom to have an open mind,

Freedom that never ends,

Freedom to enjoy yourself,

Knowing that it doesn't offend.

Freedom to feel completely safe,

Freedom to be in control,

Freedom to go in the direction you want,

Because it's good for your soul.

Freedom to love whoever you wish,

Freedom of choice,

Freedom to express yourself,

And have others hear your voice.

Freedom to not conform,

For freedom is no sin,

Freedom cannot be given or taken away,

Because freedom comes from within.

You

You make me smile,

Always on my mind,

Your voice so gentle,

Your words so kind.

Speaking with feelings,

Expressing love and care,

I only have to close my eyes,

To see you standing there.

Wanting you near me,

To feel your soft touch,

Our bodies close together,

I yearn for this so much.

But....

We must take care,

To keep this moment pure,

For it's friendship not lust,

That will eventually endure.

Future and Past

Think back to when your time began,

Think back to when you could not talk,

Remember when you were young,

Defenceless and unable to walk.

Remember when you felt safe,

Remember when all was good,

Look now, through adult eyes,

And recall your childhood.

Look now and see your children,

Look how they grow day by day,

See love on their blameless faces,

As you sit and watch them play.

In time they will copy your deeds,

In time their actions will be cast,

Believing that you were sincere,

Their future lies within your past.

Future or Past?

Pick a day from your future,

Pick a day from your past,

Which one would you prefer,

If you could make it last?

Would you chose to go back,

And relive or undo?

Would you chose to go forward,

And forget all that you knew?

To a life yet discovered,

Where everything is new,

And your past is erased,

So you, would not be you.

Gently

If we can both see the moon,

Then we are never far apart,

Hold it gently in your hands,

For it reflects my heart.

God's Work

I do God's work almost every day,

I do God's work and expect no pay,

I do God's work but why should I,

Do God's work on the day I die?

When I do God's work, I feel so great,

When I do God's work I don't feel hate,

When I do God's work, why do I,

See so many people, who are so work shy?

Good and Evil

A daily battle for these two,

Evil mind against good heart,

With winners not up to you,

Do you even play a part?

Your body is the battle ground,

Control for today the spoils,

Heart tries to talk mind round,

But your mind just recoils.

What advantage has he?

Over heart so diplomatic,

You cannot reason with me,

I am irrational and erratic.

Happiness

My happiness lies in my future,

My happiness lies in my past,

My happiness lies with others,

Who decide if it should last.

Goodbye

Abandoned and left all alone,

So lonely,

Abandoned for the rest of time,

Despair,

Abandoned by the ones you love,

So empty,

Abandoned feelings intertwined,

Laid bare,

Abandoned without precious love,

So painful,

Abandoned grieving one more loss,

Unfair,

Abandoned feeling so much pain,

So wounded,

Abandoned wanting sweet release,

No care

Grieve

Grieve for those lost and those never found,

For those never buried and those drowned,

Grieve for those you know and those you do not,

For some never felt the warmth,

Of their prepared cot.

Grieve for those born still and those never here,

For those never born and always held dear,

Grieve for those taken and those held above,

For they never felt the might

Of their Father's love

Grieve for those gone and those out of sight,

For those never arrived to see a day of light,

Grieve for those "God" shuns and those He harms,

For they never made it to the safety

Of their Mother's arms.

Healing

When you have seen death,

And been unable to breathe,

As you held them so tight,

And still watched them leave.

When you have faced death,

And yet lived to tell the tale,

As you had lost all hope,

Travelling death's destructive trail.

When you have touched death,

And yet breathed once more,

As you were unable to see,

And had your sight restored.

When you have caused death,

And know what you have done,

As your damaged wings retracted,

And the healing just begun.

Hearts and Minds

(Put your heart first)

Follow your heart and not your mind,

For your mind is not your own,

Follow your heart and not your mind,

Ignore doubting seeds that are sown.

Your heart is always pure and true,

Your mind is moulded by others,

Your heart is always pure and true,

Ignore the mind that smothers.

Your heart is your guide to your destiny,

Your mind is a distracting force,

Your heart is your guide to your destiny,

As you try to stay on course.

Your heart will be heavy if you stray,

Your mind will think it's won,

Your heart will be heavy if you stray,

But its work has just begun.

Your heart makes you ill to make you better,

Your mind makes you ill to control,

Your heart makes you ill to make you better,

So you learn what is good for your soul.

Your heart says stay to fight,

Your mind says death has no pain,

Your heart says stay to fight,

This struggle feels insane.

Your heart knows what you need,

Your mind creates confusion,

Your heart knows what you need,

Escape is just an illusion.

So ….

Follow your heart and not your mind,

For your mind is not your own,

Follow your heart and not your mind,

Ignore doubting seeds that are sown.

My mind tells me to depart,

My heart yearns to stay,

My mind tells me to depart,

My heart has won today.

Heaven and Hell

Heaven and Hell,

Is only spiritual,

Earth and skies,

Open your eyes.

Hide and Seek

Your heart is stronger,

Your mind is weaker,

Your mind hides the truth,

Your heart is the seeker.

Honour

Out of love and into hate,

Because....

All is lost and it's too late,

To change.

Tried so hard and gave my all,

But.....

You drained me with your wall,

Of silence.

With every lie that passed your lips,

You.....

Left my heart torn and ripped.

No longer will I cry for you,

For....

I am a free man amongst the few,

Of honour.

Hot Buttered Toast

Why deny yourself, hot buttered toast?

Why try to extend, the distance to your grave?

Life is about enjoyment and not living the most,

Become a master of your time and not the slave.

Why deny yourself a good bottle of wine?

If a glass is good for you, a bottle must be great,

Life is about enjoyment, that's not half full,

It's about what's in your glass as well as on your plate.

However

However you decide to cope,

However you see it through,

However bad you think it is,

You can always rely on you.

However tall the mountain seems,

However big the task,

However much you doubt yourself,

Is that the question you should ask?

However you search for answers,

However much you seek,

However much your berate yourself,

You have the strength to reach the peak

I am Not

I am not the man I should have been,
Through no fault of my own,
I am not the father I could have been,
Two seeds that I have sown

I am not the husband I used to be,
For ten and seven years,
I am not the man who used to be,
With anger, pain and tears.

I Close My Eyes

I close my eyes,

And picture myself in a green meadow,

The sun is shining and the sound of river caresses the ears,

As it flows gently past the weeping willows,

I am lying on a picnic blanket in the shade,

The temperature is perfect,

And my beautiful Barham is lying next to me,

He rests his head upon my chest,

As the gramophone plays relaxing music,

The white wine chills in the ice bucket,

As we relax, happy and content.

A solitary cloud moves slowly across the blue sky,

Butterflies and bees meander from flower to flower,

A gentle breeze brushes against us as we lie together,

Our white linen clothes and the shade keep us cool,

Our shoes rest on the riverbank,

The only witnesses to our earlier paddle.

The sounds of a propeller driven plane,

Interrupts the distant silence,

We look into each other's eyes,

And do not need to say anything,

For our eyes tell us all we need to know,

That we are deeply in love.

Mosaics

We are fragile unfinished mosaics,

Oh, how very slowly we grow,

Piece by piece we take form,

Forged from our feelings,

We spiral forever outwards,

Shaped around our souls,

And melded with memories,

Made from all our yesterdays.

I Pray

By day,

A knight,

With sword,

To fight.

By night,

I pray,

To last,

The day.

I Wonder

I wonder what I have done?

That God should smile upon me,

And bring the two of us together,

He has truly created something beautiful,

I know that we have Gods' blessing,

For he is all seeing,

He is all knowing,

And he smiles on us both.

In My Arms

Baby, when I feel down,

I close my weary eyes,

And I picture you in my arms,

The two of us in a loving embrace,

Standing in our home,

Together at last.

It is this vision,

That keeps me going,

Because I know in my heart,

That day will come,

And we will be so very happy,

I love you with all of my heart.

Innocence

Look into the eyes of a child,

They are so pure and clear,

Listen to their laughter,

What is it that you hear?

Insanity

Living in the dragon's lair,

Hiding from the tortured stares,

Mind full of insanity,

Always hoping to be free.

Journey

We are tourists of the present,

Led by ghosts of our past,

Towards a future of uncertainty,

On a journey that doesn't last.

Know

Talk of good times,

And not sorrow,

But know that sorrow exists,

Think of memories,

That you do not borrow,

But know what you will miss.

The Library of Your Mind

Books of emotion all fall out,

Words spill across the floor,

Like a bursting suitcase,

Your mind can hold no more.

As you fight to keep it in,

The volumes tumble out,

Silently you scream for help,

Inside you start to shout.

Take time to store your episodes,

For this is not a race,

Discuss the chapters of your life,

With friends and no disgrace.

Share the heaviest of paragraphs,

And one day you will find,

That you alone possess the key,

To the library of your mind.

Life is a Gift

Life is a gift,

So why do we seek,

An artificial high,

To an imaginary peak?

Falsely labelled treasure,

Stops us from seeing,

The we should gain pleasure,

From simply being.

Life

Life is not one long book,

It is a series of short stories,

Enjoy your part in each one,

Learn and move on to the next,

With dignity and enthusiasm.

Live

Write of love,

Write of truth,

Write of fairness,

Write of honour,

Write of passion,

Write of loyalty,

And compassion,

Write of all these things,

But know,

That unless you live them,

They are worthless pen marks,

On a meaningless page,

of your life.

To Grow

In order to grow you must,

Look back to the past,

Live in the present,

And

Dream of the future.

Do not live, as most will…

Always looking to the future,

Living back in the Past,

And

Dreaming in the present.

Let Yourself In

The keys that I give you,

Are more than for my home,

The door to my heart is wide open,

So tread softly when you roam.

Love

It's in the way you look,

It's in the way you smile,

It's in everything you do,

Even for a while

It's in the way you move,

It's in the way you say,

It's in everything I feel,

Each and every day

It's in the way you breathe,

It's in the way you sigh,

It's in everything you are,

And only I know why

It's in the way you touch,

It's in the way you kiss,

It's in everything I see,

And all that I miss.

A Loving Embrace

We fell asleep as lovers,

In a loving embrace,

As one, in each other's arms,

Content and face to face.

We were asleep as lovers,

When I stirred upon this night,

And gazed at you in wonder,

So beautiful a sight.

You were asleep my love,

Like an angel in my dreams,

My eyes smiled in adoration,

But you would not have seen.

You stayed asleep my love,

So completely at rest,

As I caressed your hair,

And lay my head upon your chest.

You smiled in your sleep my love,

So loving and so true,

As I kissed your tender lips,

And whispered.....

"I Love You"

Madness

Distress and madness intertwined,

Divert my thoughts to utter confusion,

The pain and anguish suffered in my mind,

Is surely far too real, just to be an illusion.

Me and You

I have a beautiful dream,

A dream that's pure and true,

A dream of love and happiness,

A dream of me and you

I see a wonderful future,

A future that's pure and true,

A future of joy and laughter,

A future for me and you.

Meant to Last

A love this strong,

Knows no distance,

A love this strong,

Knows no apart,

A love this strong,

Is so resilient,

Because,

A love this strong,

Is meant to last.

Mind of Ice

We are all skating on a frozen lake,

Never knowing when it may break,

When the pressure starts to matter,

Your mind of ice will surely shatter.

The freezing darkness takes its toll,

You cannot see the exit hole,

As you strain to see through the ice,

You become another sinking sacrifice.

How deep does it get?

Have you reached the bottom yet?

Struggling to see the helping hand,

Offering prescriptions for dry land.

Why is it such a deliberation?

To take or not this medication,

You are changed and not the same,

There are new rules to this game.

Look at yourself in a different light,

Are you sure that you're alright?

You must see yourself as ill,

For you to swallow this hard pill.

Read the instructions on the packet,

This is a medicinal life jacket,

It takes some time to fully inflate,

Just try to float, you cannot skate.

Slowly you can see the way back out,

Breaking through all of the doubt,

The fresh air tastes oh so sweet,

But take your time in getting to your feet.

Friends and family nothing planned,

With all their loving, help you to stand,

Join others skating towards the edge,

Too much for you on this thin ledge?

Skate gently at your own pace,

Wish it past but you cannot race,

Reach for where the ice is stronger,

So you can deal with more for longer?

Your skating limits, set them well,

Or you will return to your watery cell,

Tread carefully on your thin floor,

Or your mind of ice might start to thaw.

My Baby

To watch my baby suffer,

To see you in such pain,

To be able to do nothing,

Drives my mind insane.

To know that it is my fault,

That we are so far apart,

To be unable to comfort you,

Tears holes in my loving heart.

To be without you baby,

Is the worst time of my life,

I am so very sorry,

My baby, my love, my wife.

My Funeral

Let me hear your laughter on this happy day,

Let me see your smiles on faces so grey,

Let me feel your joy for a life that's passed,

Let me enjoy this party, as it's my last!

My Love

(Barham)

I kissed you while you slept,

For you looked so serene,

I kissed you while you slept,

And you would not have seen,

My smile of adoration

I kissed you while you slept,

But it was more than just a kiss,

I kissed you while you slept,

Because I could not miss,

A chance to show my love,

I kissed you while you slept,

As I gently stroked your hair,

I kissed you while you slept,

Savoring this moment's tender care,

To study your beauty

I kissed you while you slept,

But you would never know,

I kissed you while you slept,

Because I had to let it show,

How much I love you.

My Share

I crave true love and affection,

All I seek is my own reflection,

Nothing more than my fair share,

Of tender, heartfelt, loving care.

My Sister - Caroline

Living as children together,

Then growing a distance apart,

You are always and forever,

The blood in each beat of my heart.

Know that if you ever need me,

I am always right by your side,

Happiness will be yours to see ,

With your family as your guide.

I will never leave you behind,

I have seen the path of the few,

Others may pretend to be kind,

But your brother is always true.

My Vision

I have a perfect vision,

The sight of flawless beauty,

The sound of an angel singing,

The aroma of wonderful roses,

The flavour of intense passion,

The feeling of tender love.

The sight of flawless beauty,

For many the eternal goal,

I see it deep within your eyes,

Through the windows of your soul.

The sound of an angel singing,

Is in everything I hear,

That passes over your sweet lips,

When you speak to me my dear.

The aroma of wonderful roses,

Surrounds me like your love,

For you were truly sent to me,

From the heavens up above.

The flavour of intense passion,

Dances wildly on my tongue,

When we are close my darling,

And joined together as one.

The feeling of tender love,

Dries my stream of tears,

Giving me the strength I need,

To face all of my fears.

I have a perfect vision,

So completely pure and true,

It's my source of inspiration,

Because my love, it's you.

Nature Comforts Me

Nature comforts me with peaceful tranquillity,

Mother Earth smiles, a loving embrace,

Her warm bosom caresses my face,

I am truly touched by the breeze,

That sways the grass and moves the trees,

I look beyond what most see,

I am one, in complete serenity.

New Beginnings

Look deep within yourself,

What is it that you see?

Turmoil and destruction?

Or peace and tranquillity?

If you fight to stay on a path,

Then it is not meant to be,

See the signs that guide you,

And embrace your destiny.

Only Me

No one but me, knows the life I lead,
No one but me, knows what makes me bleed,
No one but me,

No one but me, can see how I feel,
No one but me, can tell false from real
No one but me,

No one but me, lies awake at night,
No one but me, lies about my plight,
No one but me,

No one but me, sees into my thoughts,
No one but me, sees the battles I've fought
No one but me,

No one but me, fights on all alone,
No one but me, fights fire with stone,
No one but me,

No one but me, knows that I will never mend,

No one but me, knows when it will all end,

Only me.

Political Rhetoric

To care for all,

With hate for none,

Truly inclusive,

But only for some.

Now is My Time

I feel so strong,

And why?

Because the last weight,

The heaviest of them all,

That was pulling me under,

Has been cut away,

Now is my time,

I can tread my own path,

Free at last,

From my tortured past.

No more must I hide,

My good deeds and bad,

I can now be proud,

Of the life that I have had.

Oh Little One

Oh little one so small,

Why did God have to call,

Your innocent soul away,

Before you saw one day.

The love from us all,

Is no less or small,

And I want you to know,

That we all love you so.

Oh little one so small,

Why did God have to call,

Your innocent soul away,

Before we had a chance to play.

My lovely angel on high,

This is farewell and not goodbye,

At this time and in this place,

Mummy and Daddy give you a loving embrace.

Oh little one so small,

Why did God have to call,

Your innocent soul away,

Now is the time for us to say.....

Mummy and Daddy Love You So Very Much.

See the love on your Mum and Dad's face,

As you rest in your final place,

We both tuck you in and kiss you goodnight,

As God's hand turns out your light.

R.I.P. Lou Reed

On this perfect day,
In this magic moment,
His pale blue eyes,
Depart this satellite of love,
Forever changed.

Play no sad song,
As the soul man drifts,
Towards the white light/white heat,
He whispers, I'm so free,
No more vicious street hassle for me.

Peace

The inner peace, that we all eventually seek,

Where no phone rings and no one speaks,

Where we all have time, to sit and contemplate,

All of the world's wonders and our own fate.

Peter (Imbert)

You are so well regarded,

And rather highly thought,

The masses who know you,

Are both touched and distraught.

You are not forgotten,

Draw strength from friends unknown,

For you have them in thousands,

And never stand alone.

Kindest regards.

Tim (Met)

Pits and Gates

I have been plunged into the pits of despair,

I have touched the fiery gates of hell,

I considered wandering in there,

But was saved by an angel.

(Thank you Wilf)

Do you Reap What you Sow?

For some it is true,

They reap what they sow,

But for others, you know,

There is nowhere to go.

Umbilical cut,

Hands tied with first breath,

All doors firmly shut,

Innocence meaningless.

Apologising,

As soon as they can talk,

Marching to the beat,

From their first walk.

Anything to please,

Will never be quite enough,

Waiting to finally leave,

But at sixteen, it will be tough.

Recharge the Soul

You don't know what I've done,

You don't know where I've been,

You don't know what I've become,

Because of what I've seen.

You don't know what I think,

You don't know how I feel,

You don't know how far I had to sink,

Before I could start to heal.

Richer or Poorer

If you have nothing but love,

Then you are rich indeed,

If you possess everything but love,

Then you are undoubtedly poor,

I know love is the key,

But where is the door?

Ripples

The river is my sanctuary,

For it reflects my soul,

Calm and tranquil on the surface,

But strong currents run below.

The Safety of a Mother's Arms

Grieve for those lost and those never found,

For those never buried and those drowned,

Grieve for those you know and those you do not,

For they never felt the warmth,

Of their prepared cot.

Grieve for those born still and those never here,

For those never born and always held dear,

Grieve for those taken and those held above,

For they never felt the might,

Of their Father's love

Grieve for those gone and those out of sight,

For those never arrived to see a day of light,

Grieve for those God shuns and those he harms,

For they never made it to the safety,

Of their Mother's arms.

Salvation

The walls that keep me in,

Are closing around my mind,

Pressing on my every thought,

With madness intertwined.

The bars that keep me here,

Are imprinted on my skin,

My freedom is dependent,

On salvation from within.

Selfish to Survive

Do not lean on me,

You are not my responsibility,

I do not have the energy,

To save you as well as me,

I must be selfish to survive,

If I'm to keep myself alive.

Shine

Is it wrong to shine like a star?
Is it wrong to trust your friends?
Is it wrong to be proud of who you are?
Although your existence offends

Is it right for you to dim your light?
Is it right for you to lie?
Is it right for you to hide from sight?
For some would have you die

Is it wrong to love another man?
Is it right for you to be alone?
Is it wrong to walk hand in hand?
With the fear of being stoned.

It is right that I should stand tall,
It is wrong to suffocate me,
It is right that I should make the call,
To Love, To Live and be Free.

Silent Screams

Deepest darkest thoughts laid bare,

Spreading through a darkened mind,

Searing tracks that brand and tear,

In hidden torture so unkind.

Deepest darkest thoughts so cold,

Freezing like the mountain streams,

His hypothermic mind unfolds,

Crying out with silent screams.

Soldiers

Soldiers on the search for peace,

Lay an endless stream of wreaths,

Hoping that when the war is won,

The loss, has saved daughter and son.

Probably Alive

When you have something to say,
But not the voice to say it,
When you have music to play,
But not the instrument to play it,
When you have a life to weigh,
But not the skill to weigh it,
Then you are probably alive today,
Not that you would know it.

Stay Young with the Young

With the passing of time,

There is less laughter,

Slowly, grain by grain,

The sand continues to drain,

Until smiles are a forgotten pastime,

And as our glass empties,

Joy gives way to pain,

And familiarity forges the chain,

That keeps contempt in its place,

Boredom is merely the beginning,

Stay young and sing outside in the rain,

Stay young, live, laugh, love and smile again.

Stream of Love

My heart you have taken,

Keep what you stole,

I want it to pleasure you,

In mind, body and soul.

Water my heart with love,

For it's a perfect fit,

For the hole in your life,

I so gladly give it.

Stream of love gently flowing,

Or my heart surely dries,

Nothing left to moisten it,

But the tears from my eyes.

I fear the salty water,

For it damages my heart,

It would slowly wither,

And we would surely part.

But....

What you do to me,

The way you make me feel,

This is beyond mere love,

This transcends what's real.

We have the same hopes,

So you see my dear,

Our love is everlasting,

Because we share our fear.

Strength

Do not allow yourself to drift,

Do not go with the flow,

Do not allow society to smother,

The way you wish to grow.

Intelligence is not measured in words,

Wealth is not measured in gold,

Your deeds do not go unnoticed,

Have the strength to be bold.

Grange Road, Sutton

The warmth of the sun,

The coolness of the breeze,

The smell of cut grass,

The swaying of the trees,

The colour of the flowers,

The blueness of the sky,

The loneliness of the cloud,

As it strolls casually by.

Take My Hand

Take my hand,

And trust me,

With your heart.

Take my hand,

And you'll see,

We'll never part.

Take my hand,

And tell me,

That you're mine.

Take my hand,

And walk with me,

For all time.

Tears of Tomorrow

Why is it,

That on any given day,

I can feel a terrible loss,

My eyes fill,

I am close to tears,

Yet,

I am unable to explain,

The source of all this pain.

There is nothing,

Anyone can do,

On this given day,

No words,

That they can possibly say,

To bring relief,

From this stealer of minds,

This in-discriminatory thief.

I am lost,

Swimming in a sea,

Of unknown sorrow,

Created by the salt water,

Tears of tomorrow.

The Angel of Death

When the grim reaper calls,

I will hug him at the door,

As my soul finally falls,

And I lose the will for more.

When my own future stalls,

I will go quietly on that night,

As darkness finally falls,

And I am called into the light.

When my sheets turn to palls,

I will relinquish gathered pain,

As the scythe finally falls,

And I am returned to earth again.

The Battle

I have come a long way,

Yet travelled no distance,

I have pushed myself,

Yet found no resistance.

I have expanded my mind,

Yet I'm not big-headed,

I have become more stable,

Yet not been unsteadied.

I have grown in stature,

Yet gained no height,

I have won the battle,

Yet had no fight.

The Few

When you have known death far too well,

But chosen to live,

When you have known loss far too well,

But still chosen to give

When you have known suffering far too well,

But chosen to heal,

When you have known pain far too well,

But still chosen to feel

When you have known lies far too well,

But chosen to stay true,

When you have known betrayal far too well,

But still chosen to be you….

Then you are truly a man amongst the few.

The Injured Child

Today I tripped and fell,

On things I never saw,

The injury that I sustained,

So painful and so raw.

Feelings of despair,

Surged through my injured mind,

I looked around for anyone,

For someone to be kind.

My painful thoughts continued,

My eyes began to fill,

A bath about to overflow,

My tears to overspill.

I needed someone to help,

I could not cope alone,

The healing words of love,

So warm and soft in tone.

Someone special touched me,

A compassionate connection,

Giving warmth from their love,

And power from their affection.

They gave me the strength,

To get back on my feet,

Pain returned to the shelf,

Of life's library so discreet.

Who was it who came?

Who helped me to recover?

Was it my Mum or my Dad?

No it was my lover.

For I am an adult,

With no need to impress,

Everyone needs help sometimes,

With their emotional distress.

The Key

Longevity is not the key,

For this is not the place to be,

Do not grieve for me.

The Life

The Day,

The night,

The darkness,

The light.

The light,

The shade,

The free,

The made.

The made,

The fear,

The silent,

The here.

The here,

The now,

The voice,

The row.

The row,

The shout,

The exit,

The doubt.

The Living Room

Only their faded pictures remain,

Casually reflecting happiness,

When all you can feel is the pain.

Only their shadow lingers still,

Where they warmed in the sunshine,

But you can only feel the chill.

Only the silence of loss is here,

Their familiar voice replaced,

By the echo of each new born tear.

Only the memory of their last breath,

Is etched eternally in your mind,

In this living room touched by death.

The End

The drowning man,

He has no friends,

So when he dies,

It is the end.

The Lonely Man

He cuts a lonely figure,

Sat high upon the hill,

The wind does not blow,

But he feels the chill,

Of loneliness.

His thoughts so unkind,

Reach deep into his soul,

And fill his weary mind,

With memories they stole,

Of sadness.

He understands the pain,

Of this suffered reality,

But that makes it no easier,

For him to finally see,

This is goodbye.

The Perfect Start

The perfect day,

The perfect night,

The perfect person,

To hold tight.

The perfect time,

The perfect touch,

The perfect person,

To love so much.

The perfect smile,

The perfect hair,

The perfect person,

To be there.

The perfect reason,

The perfect rhyme,

The perfect partner,

For all time.

The Phoenix

How does a good man make amends,

For taking a life that should not end?

How does a good man live again,

After breaking this, the sixth of ten?

How can a life so pure and white,

Fade into darkness and out of sight?

How can a man so pure and true,

Almost die, to find out he is you?

How will this phoenix rise up high,

Past her fresh ashes, drifting on by?

How will this phoenix soar once more,

With damaged wings, for his last encore?

The Polite Bird

Move a little bit closer,

Said the spider to the fly,

Because you are on the edge,

And I'd hate to watch you die

Thank you for your caring words,

I am rather near the drop,

But if it's okay with you,

I'll stay where I am and hop

The fly jumped up and down,

The web was his trampoline,

The spider was thrown around,

As he made his larder clean

The spider slowly walked in,

But his head was very sore,

From all the noise the fly made,

As he hopped and buzzed some more

Settle down, there's a good chap,

Said the spider to the fly,

You will never get away,

However hard you may try

I need to use your bathroom,

Please, He replied in mid hop,

You can see my legs are crossed,

That is why I cannot stop

The fly buzzed and hopped so hard,

To try and get himself loose,

The Spider moved closer still,

As he weaved the fly his noose

The spider was moving in,

And the fly could see his glee,

When suddenly he was gone,

As a bird took him for tea

What a polite bird that was,

Taking the spider for tea,

I hope he has a good time,

And leaves a few crumbs for me

The Storm

My past is so intrusive,

It causes me such pain,

My future such a worry,

Soaks my mind, like rain

Each tiny drop a thought,

Pulling me to and fro,

Between days already gone,

And days yet to go

Thunder and lightning of confusion,

Cloud both my weary eyes,

My past beyond my reach,

My future, made up lies

But with every drop of rain,

To what does it amount?

For I control the sunshine

And make this moment count.

The Struggle

Why question birth?

When you are born,

Why question life?

When you have form,

Why question death?

When it takes all,

Why question destiny?

When it calls.

The Thief

You have many good things to do,

You have so much more to offer,

Do not sit on your lifeless hands,

Dejected and unable to bother.

Wake yourself from this numbness,

Wash off this wearisome feeling,

Do not sleepwalk through your life,

While depression does its stealing.

Things

There are things we do not wish to witness,

But we have to see,

There are things you do not wish to have,

But accept them gracefully.

There are things we do not wish to happen,

But we must learn to accept,

There are things you do not wish to hear,

But you must always expect.

There are things we do not wish to feel,

But find we have no choice,

There were times that you should have spoken,

But found you had no voice.

There are things that we do not wish to do,

But are forced by ourselves,

There are many books you should have read,

Yet they remain upon dusty shelves.

There are things we do not wish to taste,

But it is our own medicine,

There are times you should do nothing,

Except remember every sin.

There are things we do not wish to know,

But we are forced to learn,

There are people you cannot live without,

Yet you will watch them burn.

There are things in life that are not fair,

But you will find them out,

Your parents will not share their despair,

For your time will come about.

Time Devoured

Each tick of the clock,

Becomes louder and stronger,

With every beat of his heart,

The silence,

Grows longer

Seconds,

Reaped by minutes,

Reborn into hours,

A final chapter,

Almost finished,

A life,

Time devoured.

Times of Trouble

Stream of plenty,

Refill my cup of life,

While I empty out the buckets,

That are full of all my strife.

Drops of rain,

Wash away my troubled past,

While I search for happiness,

And salvation that will last.

Rays of sunshine,

Dry my tear-soaked face,

While I discharge my sorrow,

And put love back in its place.

Winds of change,

Roll the mossy stone of fear,

While I gain the strength,

To be on my own in here.

To Be Truly Free....

To cast aside,

By luck or intent,

Your self-made shackles,

Of discontent.

To struggle out,

By sheer temerity,

From your own bonds,

Of insincerity.

To break down,

By tears of undoing,

The walls you built,

Of thoughtless eschewing.

To gain release,

By seeing clearly,

The chains you made,

Have cost you dearly.

To finally let go,

By setting free,

All that ties you,

Where you do not wish to be.

Today

Do not cry for yesterday,

Do not cry for tomorrow,

Today has only just begun,

Do not fill it with sorrow.

Everything & Nothing

To have everything but the love of my life,

Is to have nothing,

To have nothing but the love of my life,

Is to have everything,

To have everything and the love of my life,

Is too much,

So I give everything else away.

Truth

The foulest stench,

That fills the air,

Is one of deceit,

Once laid bare.

More, So Much More

Mental trauma that I have endured,
Has reduced my capacity to deal,
With all but the most mundane tasks,
And the best I can do to heal,
Is merely try to forget.

Sometimes, forgetting is not permitted,
Fear and raw emotion erupt, all too real,
Yet unreal,
I will never be the same, or have again,
What this demon has deemed fit to steal.

Dragged, unwillingly, into depression,
Ripped from thoughts to forget and forgive,
Pulled away from my only salvation,
My previous life, that I try to relive,
Is as enchanting as a rainbow,
And just as illusive.

Standing, at the very gates of hell,

In utter torment and total despair,

I am apathetic, wandering aimlessly in,

I want this to stop and cannot bear,

To take any more pain and suffering,

I am lost, I am lost,

For a moment, I am lost, I do not care.

A spark of life, conscience pricked by anger,

Shouting, loud, I raged and said,

"Give me my fucking mind back!

All of it!

Get out of my fucking head,

I will not go quietly, on this night,

Or any other day, you wish me dead."

I am left, drained and woefully tired,

I must sleep deeply, in order to restore,

My current existence as a victim, a survivor,

I want to be more, so much more,

But that is enough, enough for today,

Enough for.......

Trees of Green

Keep your secrets,

Trees of green,

For no-one living,

Has ever seen,

So much pass,

And fade away,

The painful sorrow,

Of every day.

'Twas the Night Before Payday....

'Twas the night before Payday, when all thro' the house,

Not a penny was lurking, even down the couch;

The accounts were all checked by midnight, with care.

In hope that some cash would soon be there;

The children were nestled all snug in their beds,

As the migraine danced in their parents' heads,

Mum dancing in her knickers and me in me pants,

Had just settled our brains with some super Tennants,

When from the computer there arose such a flame,

I stumbled from the couch and she did the same,

Away to the window, kicking the cat, in the dash,

I threw the computer straight through the sash,

My pants were on fire, soon my ass was on show,

As the wife smacked the flames with her bra straps aglow,

When, to my wondering eyes, the cat went all weird,

Jumping out of the window, as the mouse disappeared,

Never have I seen Hismus the cat, so lively and quick,

As we peered out, with singed boobs and smouldering dick,

A man whistled, and shouted, and called us some names,

As we gathered some cushions to cover our shame,

You Drunkards! You Dancers! Naked wiggling your hips,

Your falling computer ruined my donner and chips,
Before I could warn him, or try to call,
I could see the cat, looking to break her fall.
As she gracefully dropped, flailing and trying to fly,
Twisting and turning to get a soft landing, or die,
So from the top floor flat, on the fourth floor, she flew,
With the claws fully extended and bowels full of poo,
Then in a twinkling, I recalled, she had diarrhoea,
As I heard the wet fart, that would cost him dear,
As I drew in my head, and was turning around,
Down went the door, the man came in with a bound:
He was covered sewage from his feet to his head,
And his coat, once white, was now brownish, instead:

As he turned, I saw Hismus clinging on to his back,
She looked like a shit-scared, novelty rucksack:
His eyes - how they glowed, with anger and fury,
His cheeks were bright red, brow furrowed with worry;
His dry mouth, drawn up, showed his grinding teeth,
As cat shit dripped from nose, down to beard beneath;
A solitary lump of poo, looked slightly out of place,
Amongst the watery stains, as it slid down his face,

He can't have known that Hismus was there,

As he sat down and pushed his back to the chair,

What a stupid chump, a right silly old elf,

I laughed when I saw him, almost wetting myself;

The twitch in his eye as he screamed, so annoyed,

Gave me reason to believe, the cats claws were deployed,

He thrashed about like a crazed man, near the kitchen sink,

Hismus loosened off another wet fart, and I retched at the stink.

I squeezed my fingers astride of my nose,

Hoping my sense of smell, would draw to a close,

He looked forlorn, the coat was a present from his wife,

"Please tell her what happened so I still have my life,"

He drew out his cellphone and I cleared my throat,

For a tale of pants on fire, flying cats and shit on a coat,

He heard most of the call but disappeared out of sight,

As I told her.....

Crappy Hismus took a fall, and had a good shite.

You Understand

My fellow sufferers,
Do not despair,
Salvation is at hand,
You will rise again,
Like a Phoenix,
And spread your wings once more.

You may not fly as high,
You may not fly so swiftly,
You may have damaged wings,
But trust them,
They will hold you.

And you will see more, so much more,
Flying closer to the ground,
Than those who fly in the clouds,
You have been blessed,
It may not feel like it.

But you have endured more than most,

Your mere presence is a testament,

To your strength and courage,

You look down on no one,

Not because there is no one beneath you.

But because you understand.

What is the Call?

What is our purpose?

What is our aim?

We are not here,

For material gain.

Placed on life's treadmill,

At an early age,

We are not here,

Just to earn a wage.

What is our calling?

Where do our souls lie?

We are not here,

To eat, sleep and die.

So many signs,

We did not see,

We are not here,

Just to be.

What is the calling,

That you can feel?

You are not here,

To harm but to heal.

Whatever

Whatever happens in your life,

Whatever takes its toll,

Whatever life throws at you,

Stand tall as the dice roll.

Whatever mountain you must climb,

Whatever trauma faces you,

Whatever you must overcome,

You have the strength to see it through.

Whatever hits you the hardest,

Whatever shatters you like glass,

Whatever you may think right now,

This time will always pass.

Why?

Why is my suffering not enough?

Why is my demeanour a bluff?

Why do I hate to be alone?

But need more time on my own.

Why must I fight this battle?

Why am I surrounded by human cattle?

Why did I not see the signs?

Or see the writing between the lines.

Why aren't all minds liberated?

Why are some intellectually constipated?

Why are people's minds so blocked?

Where is the key to have them unlocked?

Why do people have sight but cannot see?

Why do people have ears but cannot hear me?

Why do people have hands for touch?

But to show affection is too much.

Why do people use tongues to spread distaste?

Why is so much human life a waste?

Why is it that most of our noses,

Will smell the manure but not the roses?

Why must I distract my mind,

From awful thoughts so unkind,

Why did I not understand,

That waves will wash away the sand.

Why am I so emotionally raw?

When someone suffers, I feel it more,

The answer, my sisters and brothers,

Is that I feel the pain of others.

Words of Wisdom for Cameron & Zahra

Live in the present,

So easy to say,

But not so easy to do.

Do what makes you happy,

Life is that simple,

But we love to complicate it.

Every question does not have an answer,

So do not always look for one,

Sometimes the best thing to do, is nothing.

Do not chase money,

You will never catch enough,

Not in one lifetime.

Do not compare yourself to others,

You will either become conceited or disappointed,

Neither of which are nice.

Dare to dream,

For without dreams,

We are nothing but empty shells.

Life is too short for hate,

But is plenty long enough,

For forgiveness.

Enjoy the small things in life,

They are with you every day,

But become invisible with time.

World of Dreams

When you enter this world of dreams,

You wonder, how far will I get?

You arrive with little conception,

Remember this, your life is set.

When you make your many choices,

You should not dwell on your regret,

For you can choose to be rich in life,

Remember this, your life is set.

When you travel different highways,

You have enough time to forget,

That you have been here before,

Remember this, your life is set.

When you've taken every turning,

And all your crossroads have been met,

You have fulfilled your destiny,

Remember this, your life is set.

Wretched Hole

Demented mind or tortured soul,

Who has dug this wretched hole?

Deepest trench as black as coal,

Who has dug this wretched hole?

Emotions of an orphaned foal,

Who has dug this wretched hole?

The daily struggle takes its toll,

Who has dug this wretched hole?

No longer will I play this role,

Who has dug this wretched hole?

Struggling up this greasy pole,

Who has dug this wretched hole?

Mind and body I cajole,

Who has dug this wretched hole?

A glimpse of daylight is my goal,

Who has dug this wretched hole?

Loved ones trying to console,

Who has dug this wretched hole?

Look at your hands as black as coal,

You have dug this wretched hole!

And.......

You are the wretched mole!

Stop fucking digging and take control,

Use all of your strength to fill this hole,

And heal your mind, body and soul.

Barham

You make me so happy,

That I smile on the inside,

Every day you are in my life,

The sun shines brighter,

The birds sing sweeter and.....

You alone, make my world,

So full of love.

You are so special to me,

Know that whatever you ask,

Could never be too much,

Anything that you desire,

That is within my power,

Is yours.......

204

You have my love,

My respect,

And my heart.

I love you so much.

You are My Life

You are the thoughts in my mind,

You are the focus of my sight,

You are the water in my tears,

When I think of you at night.

You are the air in my breath,

You are the blood inside of me,

You are the beat of my heart,

My beautiful wife to be.

You are the beauty of my day,

You are the love of my life,

You are the centre of my universe,

You are my entire life.

Your Heart so Pure

You are my red rose,

Your petals so delicate,

Your form so divine,

Your body so passionate,

When it touches mine.

You are my sweet rose,

Your lips so soft,

Your body so right,

Your scent so arousing,

When I hold you tight.

You are my dream rose,

Your dancing so erotic,

Your kisses so sweet,

Your touch so sensual,

When I sweep you off your feet,

You are my perfect rose,

Your mind so beautiful,

Your actions so true,

Your heart so pure,

When you say I love you.

Your Love

You are my first thought in the morning,

You are my last thought at night,

You are always with me,

My sun, my moon, my light.

I see how much you really care,

Your love is plain to see,

I only have to close my eyes,

To see you here with me.

I feel you're with me every day,

I see you in all that I do,

Your love is with me always,

Giving me strength to see this through.

Addiction...

Do you have a demon on your back?

Does he whisper soft havoc in your ear?

Do you find it impossible to distract,

Yourself, from all that you must hear?

Does he tempt you with treasure?

Does he insist, oh, just once more?

Does he persuade you with a pleasure,

That will leave you empty to the core?

Do you find it impossible to resist,

When he calls you to come and play?

Do you follow his shadow into the mist,

Deeper into the land of ruinous ways?

Many are the times, that you have tried,

To rid yourself of this demonic plague,

Many are the times, that you have cried,

Mercy, but your screams were far too vague.

Many are the times, that he has plundered,

Your self-esteem and your hard-earned wage,

Many are the times, that you have wondered,

Is there any release from his destructive rage?

Your demon thrives on your suffering and pain,

Starving them into submission, is the only key,

For any loss you may suffer, is their eternal gain,

And he will use it all, to bring you to your knees.

His limbs wither, with every second that you abstain,

His power shrivels, with every minute you are free,

Every hour that you give him no reason to remain,

Keeps him off your back, but he will whisper, eternally.

The Climber

Mountains, are there to be climbed,

Personal, metaphorical, real....

Or of your own irascible mind,

Mountains, are there to be climbed

Whether you are alone,

Taking on the hardest face,

Or a team on the steep incline,

Attempting to overcome or embrace,

Mountains, are there to be climbed

Where you start, is of no consequence,

Where you finish, matters even less,

For you are ultimately defined,

By each positive step of redress,

Mountains, are there to be climbed

Mountains are there to be climbed,

But not necessarily by me, personally,

I prefer to take the cable car to the cafe,

Then rest a while, that's my philosophy,

No-one said, do it the hardest way.

Rodriguez

(A Tribute)

Are you a dreamer or a player?

Is everything it seems?

Do you live the life you wanted?

Or did you prostitute your dreams?

Are you a thinker or a sayer?

Trading fact for intuition?

Do you challenge all you see?

Or peddle media repetition?

Because I've seen.....

People who think they're special,

And those who think they're unique,

But faced with reality,

We all wipe tears from our cheek.

And I've seen....

People who have nothing,

Through no fault of their own,

Forge a path in the shoes of others,

Yet never cast the first stone.

So recognise the false pain,

Of those who wailed and sobbed,

As they mislaid their own dreams,

But claimed that they were robbed.

Enlightened Times

I long to live in more enlightened times,

Where no-one chases manmade monetary tails,

I yearn to live in more pleasant times,

Where bankers mourn the loss of capitalism,

And the world rejoices to the sound of their demonic wails.

I long to live in more caring times,

Where the currency of debt, poverty and slavery are made
worthless,

I yearn to live in more loving times,

Where we are all responsible, for the wellbeing of others,

And blind eyes are no longer turned, but are cured by good
will.

I long to live in times of real freedom,

Where debt, poverty, slavery and fear, are banished to the history books,

I yearn to live in times of real happiness,

Where people flourish, because we have moved out of the shadows,

And we thrive, when we bask in the light, of our collective goodness.

Songs

Out of Love (In to Hate)

Out of Love,

In to Hate,

All is lost,

It's too late.

Every lie,

Passed your lips,

Scarred my heart,

Torn and ripped.

Listen to the words, you never said,

Listen to the song, that broke your heart,

Listen to the voice, inside your head,

Telling you, your silence, will tear you apart.

Out of Love,

In to Hate,

All is lost,

It's too late.

Tried so hard,

Gave my all,

You drained me,

With your wall.

Listen to your pain, for you have bled,

Listen to the beat, that broke your heart,

Listen to the voice, inside your head,

Telling you, your silence, will tear you apart.

Out of Love,

In to Hate,

All is lost,

It's too late.

No more tears,

Will I cry,

Standing strong,

Head held high.

(Slower)

Listen to the words, you never said,

Listen to the song, that broke your heart,

Listen to the voice, inside your head,

Telling you, your silence, will tear you apart,

Telling you, your silence will tear you apart.

(Slower)

Know your pain,

Will subside,

Every day,

You survive,

Out of Love,

And in Hate,

You are lost,

It's too late......

To change.

Listen to the Tale

Listen to the tale,
That I was sung,
For there are no problems,
Except for ones,
Created by your own mind.

And listen to your heart,
Then live to the beat,
For all of the answers,
Are at your feet...
And it's not your fault,
That you're too young,
To understand.

So listen carefully,

He whispered to me,

Some dreams will come true,

And then you'll see,

You can heal,

From anything,

That gives you wounds.

So listen to the tale,

The old man said,

Life's not about moments,

It's all about the thread,

That keeps it all together,

Sometimes the thread is young,

Sometimes it's old,

Sometimes it's fragile,

But sometimes it's gold.